Antonio Beneharo

Novena to the Holy Spirit

First edition

This book was professionally typeset on Reedsy
Find out more at reedsy.com

Contents

1.

2.

3.

4.

5.

6.

7.

8.

9.

10.

11.

12.

13.

14.

15.

16.

17.

18.

19.

20.

21.

22.

23.

24.

25.

26.

27.

28.

Preface

Let us remember that we are the Church as we start our Novena to the Holy Spirit. The Holy Spirit manifests Himself to God's people when they are gathered together. Jesus is the Head of this congregation of God's people. As we recognize that we are God's people, we also recognize our numerous shortcomings in living up to our calling, as well as our selfishness and lack of care for those in our family, neighborhood, and circle of acquaintances. We therefore start by pleading with God for forgiveness for all of our numerous shortcomings in being genuinely God's people.

1

Chapter 1

N ine days Novena to the holy spirit

Since each of us much needs the Holy Spirit's protection and assistance, we should pray and invoke Him. A man should run to Him Who is the never-ending Source of Light, Strength, Consolation, and Holiness the more he is lacking in wisdom, weak in strength, burdened with difficulties, and prone to sin. - Leo XIII, Pope.

Since it was created at the command of Our Lord Himself when He ordered His Apostles back to Jerusalem to wait for the arrival of the Holy Ghost on the first Pentecost, the novena in honor of the Holy Ghost is the oldest of all novenas. It is still the sole novena that the Church recommends. It is a forceful prayer for the light, strength, and love that every Christian so desperately needs, addressed to the Third Person of the Blessed Trinity.

The following indulgence is granted by the Church: "Partial indulgence to those who participate in a public novena before the feast of Christmas, Pentecost, or the Immaculate Conception

Although this novena can be done at any time of the year, it is customarily prayed from the Friday following

Ascension Thursday until the Saturday before Pentecost (when the Ascension is not moved to the following Sunday).

2

Chapter 2

Act of Holy Ghost Consecration

I prostrate myself in front of the vast number of heavenly witnesses and offer my body, soul, and mind to It is a forceful prayer for the light, strength, and love that every Christian so desperately needs, addressed to the Third Person of the Blessed Trinity.

The following indulgence is granted by the Church: "Partial indulgence to those who to Thee, O Eternal Spirit of God. I appreciate the brilliance of Your Purity, the unwavering Acuity of Your Justice, and the Power of Your Love. You are my soul's support and source of light. I move, live, and am in Thee. I fervently ask to be protected from committing even the smallest act of offense against Thee because I never want to cause Thee pain by disobedience to grace. Mercifully watch over every thought I have and let me to constantly be alert for and receptive to thy voice and adhere to Your kind inspirations. I cling to Thee, I devote myself to Thee, and I beg Thee, through Thy compassion, to guard me in my frailty. I beg Thee, O Adorable Spirit, Helper of my frailty, to keep me in Thy grace so that I may never offend against Thee. I hold the wounded feet of Jesus. I gaze upon His five Wounds. I cling to His Precious Blood. I adore His opened side. Give me the ability, Holy Ghost, Spirit of the Father and the Son, to perpetually and universally address Thee with the phrase "Speak, Lord / for   Thy   servant   hearth."

3

Chapter 3

P**rayer for the Seven Holy Spirit Gifts**

O Lord Jesus Christ, who promised to send a messenger before ascending to heaven. Deign to bestow the same Holy Spirit upon me in order for Him to complete in my soul the work of Your grace and love, having begun it in the souls of Thy Apostles and Disciples. Grant me the Spirit of Wisdom so that I can reject the transient things of this world and only strive for the things that are eternal, the Spirit of Understanding so that Your divine truth can illuminate my mind, the Spirit of Counsel so that I can determine the surest path to gaining God's favor and entering heaven, the Spirit of Fortitude so that I can carry the cross with Thee and to bravely face all the challenges that stand in the way of my salvation.

I pray that I will be overcome with a loving awe for God and fear offending Him in any way. Mark me, dear Lord, with the mark of Your genuine disciples, and infuse me with Your Spirit in everything I do. Amen.

4

Chapter 4

F**irst day**

Holy Spirit! Light's Lord!

Give from Thy clear celestial height, Thy unadulterated shining light!

The Spirit of God

There is only one thing that matters: eternal salvation. Sin is the only thing that should be dreaded. Sin originates from a combination of ignorance, frailty, and apathy. The Holy Ghost is a spirit of love, power, and light. He strengthens the will, enlightens the mind, and ignites the heart with God's love through His seven gifts. We should in order to assure our salvation

We should pray to the Divine Spirit every day because "The Spirit helps our infirmity." We lack the knowledge of what we ought to pray for. The Spirit, however, makes a request of us.

Prayer

Almighty and eternal God, Who has promised to regenerate us through the water and the Holy Spirit and has forgiven us of all our sins, promises to send us Thy seven-fold Spirit from heaven, including the Spirit of Wisdom and Understanding, the Spirit of Counsel and

Fortitude, the Spirit of Knowledge and Piety, and to fill us with the Spirit of Holy Fear. Amen.

Our Father (once in prayer)

Hail Mary (once in prayer)

Honor be... (7 times of prayer)

(Prayer for the Seven Gifts in the Act of Consecration)

5

Chapter 5

D_{ay Two}

Father of the Poor, come!
Come, enduring treasure!
Come, You who are the Life of All!

The Holy Fear Gift

The gift of fear makes us fearful of nothing more than offending God via sin and gives us a sovereign respect for God. It is a terror that comes from feelings of awe and filial devotion to our heavenly Father rather than from the idea of hell. The first step toward knowledge is dread, which keeps us away from earthly pleasures that can in any way cause us to drift away from God. "They that fear the Lord will prepare their hearts, and in His sight they will sanctify their souls."

Prayer

Come, lovely Spirit of Holy Fear, enter my heart from the bottom up so that I can keep Thee, my Lord and God, in front of my face always, aid me in avoiding everything that can offend Thee, and grant me the ability to stand before Thy Divine Majesty in heaven, where Thou livest and reign-est in the Blessed Trinity, God, eternally. Amen.

Daddy, we (I once prayed)

Hail Mary (once in prayer)

Honor be... (7 times of prayer)

Prayer for the Seven Gifts in the Act of Consecration

6

Chapter 6

A third day

You are the most effective comforter, visiting the distressed breast and bestowing delicious serenity.

The piety-giving gift

Our hearts develop a filial affection for God as our most loving Father as a result of the gift of piety. It encourages us to cherish and respect His Blessed Mother and the Saints, the Church and her visible Head, our parents and superiors, our nation and its leaders are all for His sake, as well as those who have been given authority by Him. When one has the gift of piety, practicing one's religion is not seen as a burdensome obligation but rather as a rewarding duty. There is no work when there is love.

Prayer

Take control of my heart, O Blessed Spirit of Piety. Therein ignite such a love for God that I would find contentment exclusively in His service and, for His sake, submit to all just authority in a loving manner. Amen.

Our Father (once in prayer)

Hail Mary (once in prayer)

Honor be... (7 times of prayer)

(Consecration Act and prayer for gifts of seven)

7

Chapter 7

Day Four

You are sweet solace in labor; pleasant cooling in the heat; and consolation in adversity.

The Ability to Be Strong

The soul is reinforced against natural dread and supported to the very end in the discharge of duty by the gift of fortitude. The will is given a push and vigor by fortitude, which inspires it to embark on the most difficult tasks without hesitation, face dangers, trample on people's respect, and bear the slow martyrdom of even lifelong tribulation without complaining. "Whoever endures to the end shall be saved."

Prayer

Come, O Blessed Spirit of Fortitude, strengthen my weakness, give me courage against all odds, uphold my soul in times of hardship and misfortune, and support my efforts toward holiness.

I'm given the gift of fortitude so that I'll never lose my faith in Thee, my God and greatest good, or be torn away from Thee. Amen.

Daddy, we (I once prayed)

Hail Mary (once in prayer)

Honor be... (7 times of prayer)

Prayer and Consecration for the Seven Gifts (I once prayed)

8

Chapter 8

D**ay Five**

Light is eternal! Luminous Divine!
Visit these hearts of Thine, and fill us to the core!

The Knowledge Gift

The soul may assess created things for what they truly are worth—in respect to God—thanks to the gift of knowledge. Knowledge exposes the pretense of animals, demonstrates their hollowness, and highlights their one and only real function as tools in God's service. It demonstrates to us God's tender care even in hardship and encourages us to exalt Him in any situation in life. We prioritize the most important things and value God's relationship above all else because of its light. "To him who possesses it, knowledge is a spring of life."

Prayer

Come, O Blessed Spirit of Knowledge, and give me the ability to understand the Father's desire. Show me the futility of earthly things so I can see their meaninglessness and utilize them solely for Thee and My own redemption, always looking ahead to Thee and Thy eternal benefits. Amen.

Our Father (once in prayer)
Hail Mary (once in prayer)

Honor be... (7 times of prayer)

Prayer for the Seven Gifts in the Act of Consecration

9

Chapter 9

Sixth day

Nothing pure in man will remain if You withdraw Your grace.

His good devolves into bad.

The Gift of Understanding

Understanding is a gift from the sacred Ghost that aids in our ability to comprehend the significance of the tenets of our sacred religion. By faith, we are aware of them, but it is through understanding that we come to value and enjoy them. It enables us to see the deeper significance of revealed truths and, via them, to experience life's newness more quickly. We start to "walk worthy of God, in all things pleasing, and increasing in the knowledge of God." Instead of being sterile and inert, our faith now motivates a way of life that offers powerful witness to the faith that is within us.

Prayer

O Spirit of Understanding, come and illuminate our thoughts so that we may understand know and believe all the secrets of salvation, and may they one day be granted the opportunity to see the eternal light in Your Light, as well as a clear view of Thee, the Father, and the Son in the light of glory. Amen.

Our Father (once in prayer)
Hail Mary (once in prayer)
Honor be... (7 times of prayer)
Prayer for the Seven Gifts in the Act of Consecration

11

Chapter 11

D_{ay Eight}

bend the heart's and will's resistance;
Warm the cold and melt the ice;
Orient the wrong-headed steps!

The Wisdom Gift

Wisdom is the most ideal of the gifts since it encompasses all the other gifts just as charity does with all the other virtues. There is a saying about Wisdom that reads, "All good things come to me with her, and innumerable riches, through her hands." Our faith, hope, compassion, and the highest level of virtue-based behavior are all bolstered, perfected, and advanced by the gift of wisdom. Wisdom enlightens the mind to distinguish and appreciate divine things, in which appreciation earthly pleasures lose their flavor and the Cross of Christ provides a savor Take up your cross and follow me, for my yoke is lovely and my burden is light, says the Savior, while the Cross of Christ produces a divine sweetness.

Prayer

Come, O Spirit of Wisdom, and make known to my soul the secrets of heavenly things, their immeasurable greatness, strength, and beauty. Teach me to love them more than all the fleeting pleasures and satisfactions of this world. Help me acquire them so I can keep them forever. Amen.

Our Father (once in prayer)

Hail Mary (once in prayer)

Honor be... (7 times of prayer)

Prayer for the Seven Gifts in the Act of Consecration

12

Chapter 12

Day Nine

Ascend in Thy seven fold blessings and soothe those who have confessed and adored Thee forever. Give them peace of mind when they pass away, eternal life with You, and unending joys. Amen.

The Holy Ghost's Fruits

The Holy Ghost's gifts enable us to practice the supernatural virtues with more docility to divine inspiration, which makes them perfect. Our service becomes more sincere and giving, and our virtuous behavior becomes more perfect as we advance in our understanding and love of God under the guidance of the Holy Ghost. These good deeds are referred to as Fruits of the Holy Ghost and fill the heart with joy and consolation. These Fruits in turn make virtue practice more appealing and serve as a potent motivator for further endeavor in God's service.

to reign is to serve Whom.

Prayer

Come, O Divine Spirit, fill my heart with Thy heavenly fruits: charity, joy, peace, patience, long-suffering, kindness, goodness, faith, mildness, modesty, self-control, and chastity, so that I may never grow weary in the service of God and may merit, by continuing to submit faithfully to Thy inspiration, to be united eternally with Thee in the love of the Father and the Son. Amen.

Daddy, we (I once prayed)

Hail Mary (once in prayer)

Honor be... (7 times of prayer)

Prayer for the Seven Gifts in the Act of Consecration

13

Chapter 13

Interceding for the Holy Spirit

Come Holy Spirit, fill the hearts of your followers and stoke the flame of your love within them. They will be produced as you send out your Spirit. And You will restore the earth's surface.

God the Father, God the Son, and God the Holy Spirit make up the Holy Trinity, which is composed of one third each. It's crucial to pray to the Holy Spirit every day. should give the Holy Spirit praise for the direction and spiritual nutrition He offers.

Catholics offer the Holy Spirit a prayer

The Holy Trinity's third Person is the Blessed Holy Spirit. You are the Spirit of holiness, truth, and love. coming from and equal to the Father and the Son I adore and worship you with all of my being. Please teach me how to seek out and know God, for whom and by whom I was formed. Fill my heart with His enormous love and a holy dread. Give me patience and humility, and keep me from sinning.

Increase my faith, hope, and charity, Holy Spirit, and help me to develop all the qualities that are appropriate for my stage of life. Help me to develop in Your seven gifts, Your twelve fruits, and four foundational virtues.

Make me a devoted and trembling disciple of Christ, a submissive member of the Church, and a helper of my neighbor. Please give me the strength to uphold the rules and achieve the sacraments with honor. Bring me to holiness in the stage of life You have called me to, and guide me through a joyful death to eternal life. via our Lord and Savior, Jesus Christ.

Give me the specific favor for which I ask name special petition as well, O Holy Spirit, Giver of all good things, if it is for Your honor and glory as well as for my well-being. Amen.

14

Chapter 14

A Prayer of Miracle to the Holy Spirit

"Dear Holy Spirit, you are the one who helps me see everything and guides me toward my objectives. You who are always by my side throughout my life and who have given me the holy gift of forgiving and forgetting the wrongs done to me. In our little call, I just wanted to say thank you for everything and reiterate my desire to never be apart from you. regardless of how strong the material desires might be. I want to be in your eternal splendor with you and my loved ones.

Amen.

15

Chapter 15

Requesting the Holy Spirit through prayer

"Heavenly Father, as Your child in Jesus, I want to fully serve as a tool for Your Kingdom to be Visible via My Life. I make an effort to fulfill your promise to provide the Holy Spirit to believers. I am baptized in the Holy Spirit by Jesus, my Savior and King. in order for the force of your resurrection to transform me in line with your purposes. Help me, Holy Spirit, and swell me to overflowing proportions. I don't withhold anything from you. Work all of your gifts through me so that the Kingdom of my heavenly Father may be made visible in and through my life. In the tremendous name of Jesus, I pray. Amen!

16

Chapter 16

An Effective Prayer to the Holy Spirit

Dear Divine Comforter, Holy Spirit!

As my True God, I worship You.

I give You glory by uniting with the prayers that the saints and angels offer to You.

I extend to You my entire heart and express my sincere gratitude.

For all the advantages You have provided for the world and continue to provide.

The source of all magical abilities is you.

Who also benefits greatly from the favors of the spirit of the Mother of God, the Blessed Virgin Mary.

I beg You to come to me through Your love and kindness and grant me the favor I have fervently requested in this novena, [Insert your wish here].

Protect our hearts, Holy Spirit, Spirit of Truth.

Shine Your light brightly onto all peoples, so they may have one religion and walk in a way that pleases You. Amen.

17

Chapter 17

Prayer for guidance

I'm pleading with the Holy Spirit for direction as I kneel in front of the enormous number of celestial witnesses. I give myself to You, Everlasting Spirit of God, body and soul. I thank You for Your radiance in Purity, Your unwavering commitment to Justice, and Your power in Love. You are the Light and the Strength of my heart.

I sincerely pray that I will never displease You by being unfaithful to Your grace, and I ask for protection from even the smallest act of disrespect toward You.

Holy Spirit, compassionately keep an eye on every thought I have and ensure that I am always alert for Your Light, attentive to Your Voice, and inspired by Your magnificent guidance. I cling to You, surrender myself to You, and beg You in the name of Your love to keep an eye out for me when I'm weak. I beg You, Sweet Spirit, Helper of My Weakness, to preserve me in Your grace so that I may never sin. I believe in the pierced Feet of Jesus. I gaze upon His Five Wounds. I cling to His Precious Blood. I adore his opened Side.

Give me the ability to say to You always and everywhere, "Speak, Lord, for Your servant heareth," O Holy Ghost, Spirit of the Father and the Son. Amen.

18

Chapter 18

P rayer for wisdom

"Heavenly Father, in the Name of Jesus, I acknowledge that as true," I pray to the Holy Spirit for wisdom. The Holy Spirit's temple is within my flesh. My faith in You is increased by my daily acceptance of Your presence. I firmly believe that You, heavenly Father, are illuminating my thoughts and leading and directing me through my spirit by the Holy Spirit.

I firmly trust that You, LORD, are directing my steps as I give myself over to the Holy Spirit. Holy Spirit, I fully commit to and believe in Your knowledge, expecting You to influence my thoughts to align with our Father's desire so that my goals will be realized and successful. I put all of my faith in You, LORD, and I do not rely on my own understanding. You guide me down the righteous way as I acknowledge You. I admit that as I grow in piety, I am better able to discern the Holy Spirit's inward testimony. Father, I hear the voice of the Good Shepherd, and I will not follow a stranger's voice. I understand that my spirit is the Lord's flame.

I don't let the WORD leave my tongue as I think about it day and night. Father, I verify my internal witness using the Word because the Word and the Spirit are in agreement. I respond quickly to the promptings of my spirit and The WORD. I am a doer as well as a listener. I am therefore blessed in everything I do.

19

Chapter 19

Personal Intercession to the Holy Spirit

"Bless you, Father "Oh, Blessed Father, how I thank You for keeping me alive in the Lord Jesus and bringing me into Your family and the Body of Christ by my faith in Him.

I am grateful that He has given me His ownership seal and made my heart His home. to uplift me on my spiritual path as He gradually changes me into the desired likeness of the Lord Jesus Christ. I ask the Holy Spirit to lead and direct me in all things and that I will have the ability to hear His gentle advice. Whenever I study Your Word or spend time in prayer with You. Please grant me the grace to recognize His stillness.

when Godly Christians are compelled to offer guidance and give me advise, as I diligently examine the scriptures each day, and the discernment to recognize Your spiritual guidance.

I ask that You provide me an open heart and a growing attitude of acceptance so that I can follow Your instructions and live a life that pleases You. I pray this in the name of Jesus, Amen, glorify my Father in heaven.

"Breathe into me, Holy Spirit, so that all my thoughts may   be   holy,"

20

Chapter 20

The morning prayer to the Holy Spirit

Holy Spirit, operate in me so that my labor can be holy as well. Holy Spirit, draw my spirit so I can only love what is holy. Give me strength, Holy Spirit, so I can stand up for everything holy.

Holy Spirit, keep me safe so that I can always be holy. enlarge our minds to comprehend the complexities of the cosmos in light of eternity.

Please lead us and help us to remain steadfast in our baptismal decision to follow Jesus' way of love on this day, Holy Spirit of good judgment and courage. Help us to recognize the true importance of justice and mercy in our daily dealings with one another, Spirit of wisdom and reverence. As we seek to resolve issues with family, nation, economy, and environment, may we value life. Our faith, hope, and love are sparked into new action each day by the Spirit of God. Infuse your presence, which permeates all of creation, with surprise and awe in our lives. Amen."

21

Chapter 21

Prayer to the Holy Spirit in the evening

"Blessed Holy Spirit, most kind Comforter, You come from the Heavenly Father in a way we cannot comprehend. I beg You to come and make yourself at home in my heart. Bless my spirit and purify and cleanse me from all sin. Save it from its evil ways, cleanse it of all impurities, wet its dryness, and warm its coldness. Make me genuinely meek and content so that I may please You and You may walk with me always.

Please enlighten me, Most Blessed and Most Kind Light. Give yourself to me, Fountain of Pure Delight, My God, Ecstatic Joy of Paradise, and kindle the flame of Your love in my deepest heart. Please guide, protect, and instruct me in everything, O Lord. Give me the ability to overcome all irrational worries and despondency. Give me an honest and complete love, a true faith, and a firm hope. Permit me to constantly follow Your Most Generous Will. Amen."

22

Chapter 22

Prayer for favor

"Holy Father, You have called me to be a temple of the Holy Spirit and a member of the mystical body of Your Son, Jesus Christ.

I beg You to provide me the understanding that comes from the Holy Spirit so I can recognize the sins of this world. Understanding, so that I may comprehend my existence and the significance behind everything in the world more fully. Counsel, that I may always make the right decision. I pray for fortitude so that I can resist temptation and remain loyal to You. Help me to adore You in everything I do, think, and say. Fear of the Lord, that if the strength of love fails me, I could be instantly made aware of the eternal repercussions of my actions. Please make your request here. Visit me by Your grace and Your love and grant me the favor I humbly ask for in this novena. Amen.

23

Chapter 23

Act of Consecration to the Holy Spirit

"Blessed Holy Spirit, Divine Spirit of light and love, I dedicate to You my understanding, heart, and will as well as the entirety of my existence for all of time and all of eternity.

May my understanding consistently follow Your heavenly inspirations and Catholic Church teaching. I pray that God and my neighbor's love will always be present in my heart. May my desires always align with Your supreme will.

May my entire life serve as a genuine illustration of the character and virtues of our Lord and Savior Jesus Christ, to whom the Father and You grant unending acclaim and glory. Amen.

24

Chapter 24

Prayer to the Holy Spirit

Welcome the Holy Spirit's Arrival

"Dear Holy Spirit, I worship you as my soul's beloved. Give me knowledge, direction, strength, and comfort. Tell me what I should do, then demonstrate how to do it. I pledge to comply with all of your requests and to accept whatever you permit to happen to me. Just make your intentions clear to me. I ask in the name of Jesus. Amen.

Prayer to Spread God's Word

Dear Lord, you have given me strength through the power of your word. My mind and heart are now more open to the miracles that You have wrought. You have given me the ability to communicate so that I can spread your holy word.

Please, Holy Spirit, guide me in comprehending the significance of these abilities and in how to make wise use of them. Bless everyone who shares the gospel through their gifts. Encourage those who work in the communications industry to put their position to use for the benefit of your people. Through the Lord Jesus Christ, I   humbly   ask   this,   Amen.

25

Chapter 25

Requesting the Holy Spirit through prayer

"Dear Holy Spirit, grant us Your seven sanctified gifts. Increase our comprehension so that we may know You. Please give us wisdom so that we can understand and accept Your will.

Please give us discernment so that we can always recognize what is right. Support us so that we can consistently be willing to carry out Your Divine Will.

Inspire us with a thirst for knowledge so that we might delve further into the realities You have revealed.

Let the innocence-filled spirit fill our hearts so that we can make You happy. Let us cultivate a proper fear of God so that we won't ever turn away from You or stray from the road.

Give us all of Your blessings so that we may exalt You. Amen.

26

Chapter 26

Encouragement Prayer

"Heavenly Father, I implore You to send the Holy Spirit. I pray that anytime I am about to forget Your law, Your Holy Spirit will prompt me. Your vows and your affection. May Your Holy Spirit help me to remember Your holiness, omniscience, wisdom, goodness, faithfulness, and love on a regular basis.

When I'm lazy, may Your Holy Spirit strengthen me. Give me strength while I'm weak. When I can no longer help myself, please help me. Blessed Holy Spirit, breathe into me so that I can act in a holy manner. Wake me up so I can love the sacred. Please fortify me so that I can protect the sacred. Holy Spirit, guard me so that you may grant me the grace I so fervently want for in this novena, that I may never lose what is holy, Amen."

Charitable Giving "Oh Holy Spirit, through Your strength, Christ was raised from the dead to save us all. Miracles are worked in the name of Jesus by Your grace. We are protected from evil because of Your love. Therefore, we humbly implore You to grant us Your gift of Charity from inside. Only your strength, Oh Divine Spirit, makes possible the tremendous charity of the host of Saints. Increase my capacity for charity so that I can love with the same generosity that the saints do. Amen."

Joy

Let us prostrate ourselves before the greatness and might of the Holy Spirit.

Let's praise the Paraclete, our advocate, and celebrate the Holy Trinity today.

Oh Holy Spirit, it was through Your might that Christ rose from the grave to redeem us all.

Miracles are worked in the name of Jesus by Your grace.

We are safeguarded from evil because of Your love.

So, we humbly and beseechingly pray for Your gift of Joy within us.

In times of adversity, difficulties, and suffering, every Saint is distinguished by an unwavering Joy.

Oh Holy Spirit, grant us the unfathomable joy so that we may live as a testament to Your love and faithfulness! Amen."

27

Chapter 27

Prayers for safe delivery

Help me, Holy One, to be brave and strong when the pain of childbirth becomes intolerable because I know You won't abandon me. Please help me to keep pushing without giving up. I thank You for your assurance that I will witness the Lord's goodness in the land of the living. I ask that You keep me safe throughout the delivery process (Joshua 1:9, Hebrews 13:5, Psalm 27:13).

I thank You, Almighty One, for Your promise—"The Lord Your God is with you, the mighty warrior who saves"— remains true as I enter the delivery room. He will be very pleased with you. I'm grateful that Your love will allay my worry and that You will be glad for me.

even though I work very hard, I sing. Dear Lord, You will keep my wife and I in complete peace throughout the delivery procedure as I put my mind on You. I ask God to protect my darling child from harm during delivery (Zephaniah 3:17; Isaiah 26:3).

Father God, I come before You in prayer for a safe delivery. I thank You for entering the delivery room ahead of me, behind me, above me, and beneath me.

Thank you for loving this child and me more than I could ever imagine. I ask that You use Your faithfulness to protect my baby during the childbirth procedure. I ask God to keep her heart, lungs, and every other small part of her body safe. Thank You for creating her in such a fearfully and wonderfully way and for planning every day of her life. I ask the Holy Spirit, the breath of God, to keep putting life in her little lungs throughout labor and delivery (Ephesians 6:15; Psalm 139:13; John 14:26), Amen.

28

Chapter 28

Holy Spirit Litany

(For private recitation)

Lord, please show us mercy. Lord, please show us mercy.

Have mercy on us, Christ. Have mercy on us, Christ.

Lord, please show us mercy. Lord, please show us mercy.

Father, you are all-knowing; have mercy on us.

Save us, Jesus, Son of the Living God and Redeemer of the World.

We are made holy by the Spirit of the Father and the Son, who both have endless life.

Hear us, Holy Trinity.

Enter our hearts, Holy Spirit, who comes from the Father and the Son.

Entering our hearts is the Holy Spirit, who is equal to the Father and the Son.

COMMENT: Please have mercy on us. Source of heavenly water, Author of all good, Ray of heavenly light, God the Father's promise, Consuming fire, and Ardent charity, spiritual unction, the Holy Spirit, that Sanctifies, the Holy Spirit who governs the Church, the Gift of God the Most High, the Spirit who fills the universe, the Spirit of the adoption, the Spirit of wisdom and understanding, the Spirit of counsel and fortitude, the Spirit of knowledge and piety, the Spirit of the fear of the Lord, the Holy Spirit of grace and prayer, the Spirit of peace and meekness, the Spirit of modesty and innocence, the Spirit of knowledge and

Holy Spirit, awaken in us a dread of sin.

Come, Holy Spirit, and let the earth's surface be renewed.

Holy Spirit, fill our souls with Your light.

Inscribe Your law in our hearts, Holy Spirit.

Holy Spirit, ignite the flame of Your love inside us.

Holy Spirit, let us have access to the riches of Your graces.

Holy Spirit, guide us in effective prayer.

Bring us Your wonderful inspirations, Holy Spirit.

Please show us the route to salvation, Holy Spirit.

Holy Spirit, give us the one and only wisdom that we need.

Holy Spirit, help us to be decent people.

Give us the benefits of all virtues, Holy Spirit.

Holy Spirit, help us to continue to pursue justice.

Our eternal prize, Holy Spirit.

Send us Your Holy Spirit, O Lamb of God, Who atones for the sins of the world.

The Holy Spirit's gifts are poured down into our souls by the Lamb of God, Who atoned for all of mankind's sins.

Grant us the forgiveness of sins through the sacrifice of the Lamb of God, Give us the Spirit of wisdom and piety, O Thou that takest away the sins of the world.

V: Holy Spirit, come! Fill the hearts of Your devoted,
R: and fan the flame of Your love within them.

Our Lord Jesus Christ, Your Son, Who with Thee, in the unity of the same Spirit, lives and reigns, one God, forever and ever, let us pray: Grant, O merciful Father, that Your Divine Spirit may enlighten, inflame and purify us, that He may penetrate us with His heavenly dew and make us fruitful in good works.

R. Amen.

Printed in Great Britain
by Amazon

21775262R00031